教材规划小组
Teaching Material Project Planning Group

许琳　夏建辉　张健　郝运

海外咨询小组
Overseas Consulting Group

洪　玮	美国普渡大学
周明朗	美国马里兰大学
王命全	美国塔夫茨大学
陈山木	加拿大不列颠哥伦比亚大学
吴小燕	加拿大多伦多大学
王仁忠	加拿大麦吉尔大学
白乐桑	法国巴黎东方语言文化学院
顾安达	德国柏林自由大学
袁博平	英国剑桥大学
吴坚立	澳大利亚墨尔本翩丽艾森顿文法学校
罗　拉	俄罗斯莫斯科国立语言大学
三宅登之	日本东京外国语大学
李充阳	韩国首尔孔子学院
朴兴洙	韩国外国语大学
希夏姆	埃及艾因夏姆斯大学

孔子学院总部/国家汉办
Confucius Institute Headquarters (Hanban)

荣获"优秀国际汉语教材奖"
Won the Award for Outstanding International Chinese Language Teaching Materials

刘珣◎主编

英文注释
Annotated in English

NEW PRACTICAL CHINESE READER

3rd Edition

CHINESE CHARACTERS WORKBOOK
汉字练习册

编 者：刘珣 王世建

新实用汉语课本

（第3版）

北京语言大学出版社
BEIJING LANGUAGE AND CULTURE UNIVERSITY PRESS

successfully with less effort invested. The radical of every character in the Chinese Characters Workbook is marked in bold to help you accumulate knowledge about radicals, deepen your understanding of the components and semantic radicals of Chinese characters, and make it easier for you to master the forms and meanings of Chinese characters.

5. Chinese characters come in both simplified and complex forms, catering to the different needs of yours. This book has different requirements regarding simplified and complex characters. For simplified characters, you are supposed to be able to both recognize and write them; for complex characters, however, you are only required to recognize them. Of course, adjustments may be made according to what your teacher requires of you.

Now, are you ready? Let's follow *New Practical Chinese Reader* and begin our journey with Chinese characters!

目录 Contents

11 我玩儿得非常高兴
Wǒ wánr de fēicháng gāoxìng
I had a great time ... 1

非 片 建
信 展 衣
玩 片 毛
又 明 发 西
吃 得 东
从 觉 懂
查 小 句
观 字 美
民 参 景 通
人 房 员
镑 业 厦
英 馆 话
排 营 么
队 哦 这
得 次 那
常 楼 裙
那 这
高
裙

12 您要寄到哪儿
Nín yào jìdào nǎr
Where do you want to send your parcel ... 15

海 填 定
空 费 通
航 邮 告 司
口 放 事
窗 称 门
后 一 专
以 右 得 办
单 完 最 辛
拿 本 套 苦
安 件 记
保 名 自
清 第 己
裹 收 版
包 运 姓 敲

13 请您把姓名和手机号写在这儿
Qǐng nín bǎ xìngmíng hé shǒujīhào xiě zài zhèr
Please write your name and cell phone number here ... 29

还 箱 概
才 趟 帽
馆 铁 次 下 接
使 车 停 地 断
把 火 走 坏
照 装 遇 便
护 印 是 络
证 复 总 方
份 交 天 网
身 生 聊 无
带 学 来 线
卡 丢
长 音
顺 乐

14 租的比买的便宜多了
Zū de bǐ mǎi de piányi duō le
Renting is much cheaper than buying ... 41

量 容 作 式 卫
商 难 写 租 丝
目 样 记 短 棉
节 意 借 出 真
演 同 分
表 打 旗 公
开 故 浅 红
会 太 水 需 深
晚 提 装 颜 色
留 服 强 选
剧 或 说 再
话 议 建
比 易 找 白 生

15 中国画跟油画不一样
Zhōngguóhuà gēn yóuhuà bù yíyàng
Chinese paintings and oil paintings are different ... 55

术 开 门 好 中 国 画 花 鸟 一 始 已 经
家 不 敢 当 油 对 感 兴 趣 京 马 虎 谦

虚	幅	法	远	在	边	近	眼	前	些	电	梯	笑
它	们	忘	主	要	墨	彩	匹	别	好	像	往	虾
书	但	介	绍									

16　Wǒ shì wǔ suì kāishǐ xué yóuyǒng de
我是五岁开始学游泳的
It was at age five that I first learned to swim　　67

减	肥	所	以	锻	炼	因	为	体	有	重	增	加	胖
运	动	踢	足	球	步	队	视	迷	游	泳	池	农	村
教	练	河	比	赛	接	当	正	外	市	精	极	上
半	场	分	下	剩				援	辅	导	差
											下	赢

17　Nǐ kànguo jīngjù méiyǒu
你看过京剧没有
Have you ever seen Beijing opera　　79

过	杂	技	组	织	著	名	古	典	部	爱	情	感
姑	娘	结	婚	痛	死	离	角	虽	然	好	听	戴
面	具	脸	谱	海	报	芭	蕾	舞	愿	意	陪	提
琴	拉	寒	假	曲								

18　Wǒmen páshang Chángchéng lái le
我们爬上长城来了
We have climbed up the Great Wall　　89

要	放	旅	游	打	算	优	色	而	且	丰	富	文
化	传	欣	赏	南	方	预	订	乡	拍	划	爬	山
顶	鸡	蛋	牛	奶	菜	来	洞	继	照	发	阴	气
温	北	帮	忙	站	起		续	终	于			

19　Qìchē bèi wǒ zhuàng le
汽车被我撞了
I crashed into a car　　99

胳	脖	被	撞	伤	检	查	重	着	就	腿	别	提	如
倒	霉	站	骑	司	机	拐	注	原	医	药	够	弯	运
果	糟	糕	躺	报	纸	桌	消	结	椅	搬	抓	钱
偷	破	财	免	灾	麻	烦	息	派	所			
气	心	因	祸	得	福	早	日	康	复			

20　Qǐng bǎ diànnǎo ná chulai
请把电脑拿出来
Please take out your computer　　113

背	靠	户	座	位	过	道	行	李	托	超	斤	登
机	牌	脑	鞋	脱	筐	瓶	哎	呀	广	播	班	巧
俩	称	呼	经	理	父	母	际	更	贸	易	机	会
越	联	系	希	望	待	了	解		务	习	惯	活
微												

11

Wǒ wánr de fēicháng gāoxìng

我玩儿得非常高兴

I had a great time

de	*a structural particle*
得	11 strokes

pái	to arrange; to put in order （排队）
排	11 strokes

duì	row of people; line （排队）
队	4 strokes

yīng	Britain （英镑）
英	8 strokes

· 1

新实用汉语课本（第3版）汉字练习册2

New Practical Chinese Reader (3rd Edition) Chinese Characters Workbook 2

bàng	pound	（英镑）

镑 — 15 strokes

rén	person	（人民）

人* — 2 strokes

mín	the people	（人民）

民 — 5 strokes

bì	money; currency	（人民币）

币 （幣） — 4 strokes

chá	to check; to look up	

查 — 9 strokes

第 11 课　我玩儿得非常高兴
Lesson 11　I had a great time

cóng	from
从 从	ノ 人 从 从　4 strokes 　　　　　從
从 从	

yòu	again
又 又	フ 又　2 strokes 　　　　　又
又 又	

wán	to play
玩 玩	ー ニ 干 王 王 玎 玡 玩　8 strokes 　　　　　玩
玩 玩	

fēi	no; not　（非常）
非 非	ノ 丨 キ 丯 丯 非 非 非　8 strokes 　　　　　非
非 非	

cháng	ordinary; common　（非常）
常 常	丨 丷 丷 尚 尚 尚 尚 常 常 常 常　11 strokes 　　　　　常
常 常	

新实用汉语课本（第3版）汉字练习册 2
New Practical Chinese Reader (3rd Edition) Chinese Characters Workbook 2

xìn	letter
信*	9 strokes

piàn	flat, thin piece; slice （明信片）
片*	4 strokes

nà	that （那儿）
那*	6 strokes

ò	(expressing realization and understanding) oh
哦	10 strokes

yíng	to run; to operate （营业）
营	11 strokes

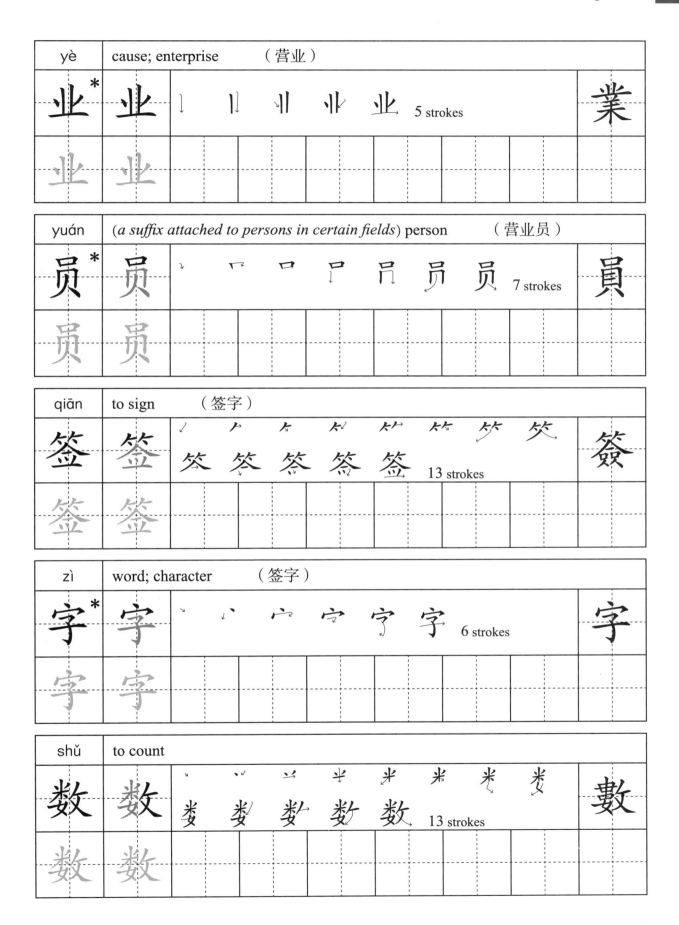

jué	to sense; to feel/sleep （觉得）
觉* 觉	丶 丷 丷 丷 ⺍ 兴 觉 觉 觉 9 strokes / 覺

de	used with "得" to form "觉得" (to feel; to think)
得 得	丿 彳 彳 彳 彳 彳 得 得 得 得 得 11 strokes / 得

fā	to develop; to expand （发展）
发 发	一 ナ 为 发 发 5 strokes / 發

zhǎn	to open up; to spread out （发展）
展* 展	一 コ 尸 尸 尸 屏 屏 屏 展 展 10 strokes / 展

jiàn	to build
建 建	フ ⺕ ⺕ ⺕ 聿 聿 建 建 8 strokes / 建

第 11 课　我玩儿得非常高兴
Lesson 11　I had a great time

| gāo | tall; high | （高楼） |

高* 高　丶 亠 宀 古 古 高 高 高 高　10 strokes　高

| lóu | building | （高楼） |

楼* 楼　一 十 扌 木 术 术 术 栏 栏 栏 桄 楼 楼　13 strokes　樓

| dà | big | （大厦） |

大* 大　一 ナ 大　3 strokes　大

| shà | tall building; mansion | （大厦） |

厦 厦　一 厂 厂 厂 厂 厍 厍 厦 厦 厦 厦 厦　12 strokes　厦

| yè | night | （夜景） |

夜 夜　丶 亠 广 广 疒 夜 夜 夜　8 strokes　夜

pinyin	meaning									
jǐng	view; scenery （夜景）									
景		12 strokes								景

měi	beautiful; pretty									
美		9 strokes								美

shāng	business; trade; commerce （商场）									
商*		11 strokes								商

chǎng	large place where people gather for a specific purpose （商场）									
场		6 strokes								場

dōng	east					东西 thing; stuff				
东*		5 strokes								東

第 11 课 我玩儿得非常高兴
Lesson 11 I had a great time

xī	west		东西 thing; stuff

西* 西 一 厂 丙 两 西 西 6 strokes 西

máo	hair; feather; down	（毛衣）

毛 毛 丿 二 三 毛 4 strokes 毛

yī	clothes; garment; dress	（毛衣）

衣* 衣 丶 二 ナ 衣 衣 衣 6 strokes 衣

qún	skirt	（裙子）

裙 裙 丶 ラ ネ ネ ネ ネ 衤 衤 衤 裙 裙 12 strokes 裙

zhè	used with "么" to form "这么" (so; such)		

这 这 丶 二 テ 文 文 这 这 7 strokes 這

me	used with "这" to form "这么" (so; such)							
么 么	ᅩ 么 么 3 strokes							麼
么 么								

huà	spoken words expressing meaning, including the written records of speech （上海话）							
话 话	ᅩ 讠 讠 诈 话 话 8 strokes							話
话 话								

pǔ	general; universal （普通）							
普 普	ᅩ 亠 亠 讠 诈 并 普 普 普 普 12 strokes							普
普 普								

tōng	common; general （普通）							
通 通	ᄀ ᄀ 甬 甬 甬 甬 通 通 10 strokes							通
通 通								

liú	to flow （流利）							
流 流	丶 冫 氵 氵 浐 浐 浐 流 流 10 strokes							流
流 流								

第 11 课　我玩儿得非常高兴
Lesson 11　I had a great time

lì	favourable; smooth　（流利）
利	利	ノ 二 千 千 禾 禾 利　7 strokes	利
利	利		

jù	sentence
句	句	ノ 勹 勹 句 句　5 strokes	句
句	句		

dǒng	to know; to understand
懂	懂	忄 忄 忄 忄 忄 忄 忄 憎 憎 憎 憎 懂 懂　15 strokes	懂
懂	懂		

12

Nín yào jìdào nǎr
您要寄到哪儿
Where do you want to send your parcel

bāo	to wrap; to envelop/parcel; package （包裹）
包* 包	ノ 勹 匀 匇 包 5 strokes 包
包 包	

guǒ	to wrap; to bind （包裹）
裹 裹	亠 亠 宀 宁 宁 宣 車 寅 東 東 裏 裏 裹 14 strokes 裹
裹 裹	

bǎo	to protect; to defend （保安）
保 保	ノ 亻 亻 俨 伊 伊 伊 保 9 strokes 保
保 保	

ān	safe; secure （保安）
安 安	丶 丷 宀 宁 安 安 6 strokes 安
安 安	

新实用汉语课本（第3版）汉字练习册2
New Practical Chinese Reader (3rd Edition) Chinese Characters Workbook 2

ná	to take; to hold; to carry
拿	10 strokes — 拿 (traditional: 拿)

dān	form; list （单子）
单	8 strokes — 单 (traditional: 單)

yǐ	used before a word of locality to indicate the time, position, etc. 以后 after; later
以	4 strokes — 以

hòu	(of time) after; afterwards; later （以后）
后	6 strokes — 后 (traditional: 後)

chuāng	window （窗口）
窗	12 strokes — 窗

第 12 课　您要寄到哪儿
Lesson 12　Where do you want to send your parcel

| kǒu | (of a container) opening | （窗口） |

口　口　丶 冂 口　3 strokes　口
口　口

| háng | to navigate | （航空） |

航　航　丿 亻 丬 月 月 舟 舟 舟 舢 航　10 strokes　航
航　航

| kōng | sky; air | （航空） |

空*　空　丶 丷 宀 宀 宀 空 空 空　8 strokes　空
空　空

| hǎi | sea | （海运） |

海　海　丶 丶 氵 氵 汇 海 海 海 海　10 strokes　海
海　海

| yùn | to carry; to transport; to ship | （海运） |

运*　运　一 二 云 云 运 运 运　7 strokes　運
运　运

| qīng | clear; distinct; pure | （清楚） |

清 — 11 strokes

| chǔ | clear; clearly | （清楚） |

楚 — 13 strokes

| biàn | a measure word for actions from the beginning to the end |

遍 — 12 strokes

| zuǒ | left; the left side | 左右 approximately; about |

左 — 5 strokes

| yòu | right | 左右 approximately; about |

右* — 5 strokes

第 12 课   您要寄到哪儿
Lesson 12   Where do you want to send your parcel

yī	used with "般" to form "一般" (ordinary; common; general)

一   1 strokes

bān	used with "一" to form "一般" (ordinary; common; general)

般   10 strokes

chēng	to weigh

称   10 strokes

fàng	to put; to place

放   8 strokes

yóu	to post; to mail （邮费）

邮   7 strokes

mén	class; category	（专门）

门 — 3 strokes — 門

pǎo	to run	

跑 — 12 strokes

gào	to tell; to inform	（告诉）

告* — 7 strokes

sù	to tell; to narrate; to relate	（告诉）

诉 — 7 strokes — 訴

dìng	to fix; to set	一定 certainly; must

定* — 8 strokes

第 12 课　您要寄到哪儿
Lesson 12 Where do you want to send your parcel

bǎn	edition
版	ノ 丿 ㇏ 片 片 片 版 版　8 strokes

dì	a prefix indicating ordinal numbers
第	ノ 广 卢 卢 ゲ 竺 竺 笃 笃 第 第　11 strokes

běn	a measure word for books, periodicals, etc.
本	一 十 才 木 本　5 strokes

tào	a measure word indicating series or sets of things
套	一 ナ 大 太 本 本 奍 套 套 套　10 strokes

kuài	fast　（快递）
快*	ノ 丶 忄 忄 忄 快 快　7 strokes

新实用汉语课本（第3版）汉字练习册2
New Practical Chinese Reader (3rd Edition) Chinese Characters Workbook 2

dì	to pass; to hand over （快递）

递 — 10 strokes — 遞

tì	to replace; to substitute for

替 — 12 strokes — 替

bàn	to handle; to deal with （办事）

办* — 4 strokes — 辦

shì	matter; thing （办事）

事* — 8 strokes — 事

wèi	*a measure word for people* (*polite form*)

位 — 7 strokes — 位

Lesson 12 Where do you want to send your parcel

第 12 课 您要寄到哪儿

gōng	public; public affairs; official business （公司）
公* 公	丿 八 公 公 4 strokes 公

sī	department （公司）
司 司	丁 刁 刁 司 司 5 strokes 司

tōng	to connect; to get through
通 通	⁊ マ ア 甬 甬 甬 甬 甬 通 通 10 strokes 通

qiāo	to knock
敲 敲	丶 亠 广 亠 亠 高 高 高 高 高 高 敲 敲 敲 14 strokes 敲

zì	self; oneself; one's own （自己）
自 自	丿 丿 亻 白 自 自 6 strokes 自

· 25

| fèn | share; part; portion | （身份） |

份 份 丿 亻 亻 伀 份 份 6 strokes 份

| zhèng | certificate; evidence | （身份证） |

证 证 丶 讠 订 订 证 证 7 strokes 證

| hù | to protect; to guard | （护照） |

护 护 一 扌 扌 扩 扩 护 7 strokes 護

| zhào | licence; permit | （护照） |

照 照 丨 冂 日 日 町 昭 昭 昭 昭 昭 照 照 13 strokes 照

| bǎ | used to indicate the object is ahead of the verb |

把 把 一 寸 扌 扩 扣 把 7 strokes 把

第 13 课 请您把姓名和手机号写在这儿
Lesson 13 Please write your name and cell phone number here

shǐ	envoy; emissary （大使）
使	8 strokes — 使

guǎn	embassy; legation; consulate （大使馆）
馆	11 strokes — 館

cái	not...until; only then; only
才*	3 strokes — 纔

huán	to return
还	7 strokes — 還

cháng	long
长	4 strokes — 長

新实用汉语课本（第3版）汉字练习册2
New Practical Chinese Reader (3rd Edition) Chinese Characters Workbook 2

| xué | to study (usually with an object) | （学生） |

学* 学 丶 丶 丷 丷 訾 当 学 学 | 學
8 strokes

| shēng | pupil; student | （学生） |

生 生 丿 亻 仁 牛 生 | 生
5 strokes

| jiāo | to give; to hand over/in; to submit |

交 交 丶 亠 六 亣 交 | 交
6 strokes

| fù | to repeat | （复印） |

复* 复 丿 亠 仁 午 白 甴 复 | 複
9 strokes

| yìn | to print | （复印） |

印 印 丿 厶 仨 印 印 | 印
5 strokes

第 13 课　请您把姓名和手机号写在这儿
Lesson 13　Please write your name and cell phone number here

zhuāng	to load; to pack; to install		
装	装	丶 丶 丬 丬 壮 壮 壮 妆 装 装 装　12 strokes	装

huǒ	fire	（火车）	
火	火	丶 丶 ⺌ 火　4 strokes	火

chē	vehicle	（火车）	
车*	车	一 七 车 车　4 strokes	車

tiě	ferrum (Fe); iron	高铁　high-speed rail	
铁*	铁	ノ 𠂉 ⺕ 年 钅 钅 钅 铁 铁　10 strokes	鐵

cì	order; ranking		
次	次	丶 ⺀ ⺀ 冫 次 次　6 strokes	次

新实用汉语课本（第3版）汉字练习册 2
New Practical Chinese Reader (3rd Edition) Chinese Characters Workbook 2

tàng	*a measure word for trips*

趟 趟 — 一 十 キ キ キ 走 走 趟 趟 趟 趟 15 strokes 趟

xiāng	suitcase; box （箱子）

箱 箱 ノ ト ト 竹 竹 竹 竹 笮 笮 箝 箱 箱 箱 15 strokes 箱

shùn	(*as opposed to "against"*) in the same direction as; with （顺利）

顺 顺 ノ 丿 川 厂 厅 顺 顺 顺 顺 9 strokes 顺

lái	*used with "后" to form "后来" (later on; afterwards)*

来 来 一 一 口 平 平 来 来 7 strokes 來

liáo	to chat （聊天儿）

聊 聊 一 厂 ｢ 戸 耳 耳 耳 耵 耵 聊 11 strokes 聊

第 13 课　请您把姓名和手机号写在这儿
Lesson 13　Please write your name and cell phone number here

tiān	sky; heaven	（聊天儿）

天　天　一 二 干 天　4 strokes　天

zǒng	always	（总是）

总　总　丶 丷 丷 䒑 兴 总 总 总　9 strokes　總

shì	to be; is/am/are	总是　always

是*　是　丨 口 日 日 旦 早 旱 昻 是　9 strokes　是

yù	to meet; to encounter

遇　遇　丨 口 日 日 日 禺 禺 禺 禺 禺 遇 遇　12 strokes　遇

zǒu	to walk; to leave

走　走　一 十 土 キ 卡 卡 走　7 strokes　走

新实用汉语课本（第3版）汉字练习册2
New Practical Chinese Reader (3rd Edition) Chinese Characters Workbook 2

fāng	used with "便" to form "方便" (convenient)
方 方	丶 一 亠 方 4 strokes 方

biàn	convenient （方便）
便 便	丿 亻 亻 仁 佢 佢 便 便 9 strokes 便

luò	something resembling a net （网络）
络 络	乙 幺 纟 纱 级 络 络 9 strokes 络

huài	bad; harmful
坏 坏	一 十 土 圡 圷 坏 坏 7 strokes 壞

duàn	to break; to stop
断 断	丶 丷 业 半 米 迷 迷 断 断 断 11 strokes 斷

38

第 13 课 请您把姓名和手机号写在这儿
Lesson 13 Please write your name and cell phone number here

jiē	to meet; to pick up; to connect									
接 接	一 † 扌 扌 扩 扩 扩 拉 挨 接 接 11 strokes									接
接 接										

14

Zū de bǐ mǎi de piányi duō le
租的比买的便宜多了
Renting is much cheaper than buying

bǐ	than
比	4 strokes

huà	word; talk; remark	话剧 modern drama; stage play
话*	8 strokes	

jù	drama; play	（话剧）
剧	10 strokes	劇

liú	to study abroad	（留学）
留	10 strokes	

· 41

| wǎn | evening | （晚会） |

晚 | 晚 | 丨 冂 冃 日 日' 日⺈ 昑 昑 昍 昒 晚 11 strokes | 晚

| huì | gathering with a specific purpose | （晚会） |

会 | 会 | 丿 人 人 仐 会 会 6 strokes | 會

| kāi | to hold (a meeting, symposium or exhibition) |

开 | 开 | 一 二 𠂇 开 4 strokes | 開

| biǎo | to show; to display | 表演 to perform |

表 | 表 | 一 二 三 丰 主 表 表 表 8 strokes | 表

| yǎn | to act; to perform | （表演） |

演 | 演 | 丶 冫 氵 氵 氵 氵 氵 氵 沪 渲 渲 渲 渲 演 14 strokes | 演

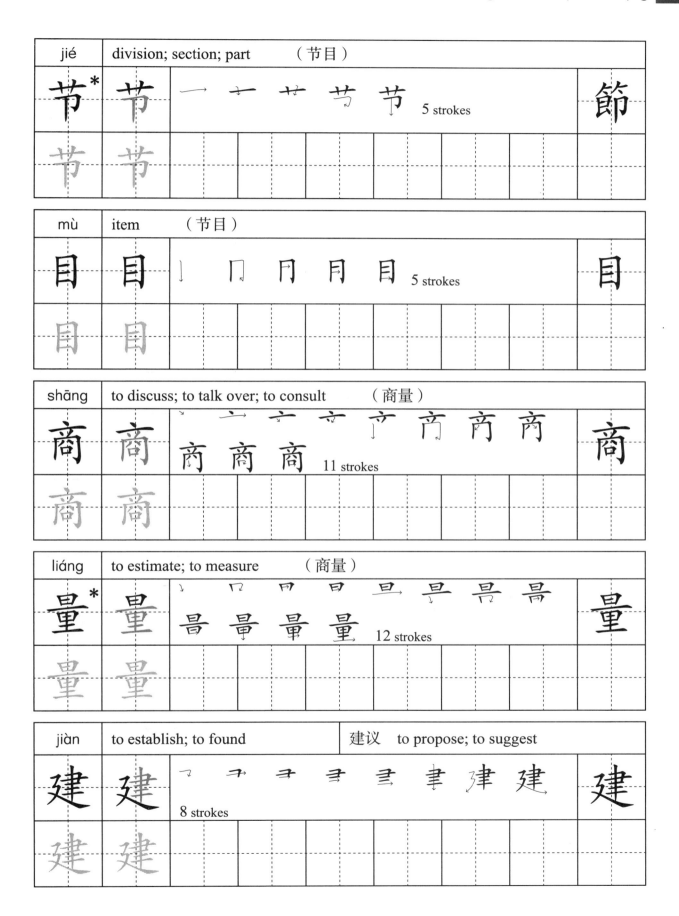

nán	difficult; hard								
难	难	10 strokes							難

róng	to hold; to contain		容易 easy						
容	容	10 strokes							容

yì	easy	（容易）							
易	易	8 strokes							易

zài	again; once more	（再说）							
再*	再	6 strokes							再

shuō	to say; to speak	（再说）							
说*	说	9 strokes							说

第 14 课　租的比买的便宜多了
Lesson 14　Renting is much cheaper than buying

tí	to lift; to raise　（提高）

提　12 strokes

shuǐ	water　　水平　standard; level

水　4 strokes

píng	level; flat; even　　水平　standard; level

平　5 strokes

gù	old; former　（故事）

故　9 strokes

tóng	same; similar; identical　（同意）

同　6 strokes

新实用汉语课本（第3版）汉字练习册2
New Practical Chinese Reader (3rd Edition) Chinese Characters Workbook 2

yì	meaning; idea; thought （同意）
意* 意	丶 亠 亣 立 产 音 音 音 意 意 意 13 strokes 意

jì	to write down; to record （记者）
记 记	丶 讠 记 记 记 5 strokes 记

zhě	used after a verb, an adjective or a phrase to indicate a class of persons or things （记者）
者 者	一 十 土 耂 耂 者 者 者 8 strokes 者

xiě	to write （写作）
写* 写	丶 冖 写 写 写 5 strokes 寫

zuò	to write; to compose （写作）
作 作	丿 亻 仁 仁 作 作 作 7 strokes 作

第 14 课 租的比买的便宜多了
Lesson 14 Renting is much cheaper than buying

zhǎo	to look for; to find

找 — 一 † † † 找 找 找 7 strokes

qiáng	(*as opposed to* "*weak*") strong; powerful; mighty

强 — 丩 弓 弓 弓' 弓' 弓' 弓' 强 强 强 强 12 strokes

fú	clothes; dress （服装）

服 —) 刀 月 月 月' 服' 服 服 8 strokes

zhuāng	outfit; clothes （服装）

装 — ㇀ 丬 丬 壮 壮 壮 壮 装 装 装 装 12 strokes

xū	to need; to require （需要）

需 — 一 广 戸 币 币 币 币 雪 雪 雪 雪 需 需 14 strokes

yào	to want; would like （需要）
要* 要	一 一 一 冂 酉 酉 要 要 要 9 strokes 要
要 要	

qí	banner, refers to the eight Manchurian administrative and military divisions （旗袍）
旗 旗	一 丁 方 方 方 扩 扩 扩 扩 旌 旌 旌 旗 旗 14 strokes 旗
旗 旗	

páo	gown （旗袍）
袍 袍	丶 冫 衤 衤 衤 衤 衤 袍 袍 袍 10 strokes 袍
袍 袍	

jiè	to borrow
借 借	丿 亻 亻 什 件 件 供 借 借 借 10 strokes 借
借 借	

duǎn	short
短* 短	丿 丿 上 仁 矢 矢 矢 矢 矩 短 短 短 12 strokes 短
短 短	

第 14 课　租的比买的便宜多了
Lesson 14 Renting is much cheaper than buying

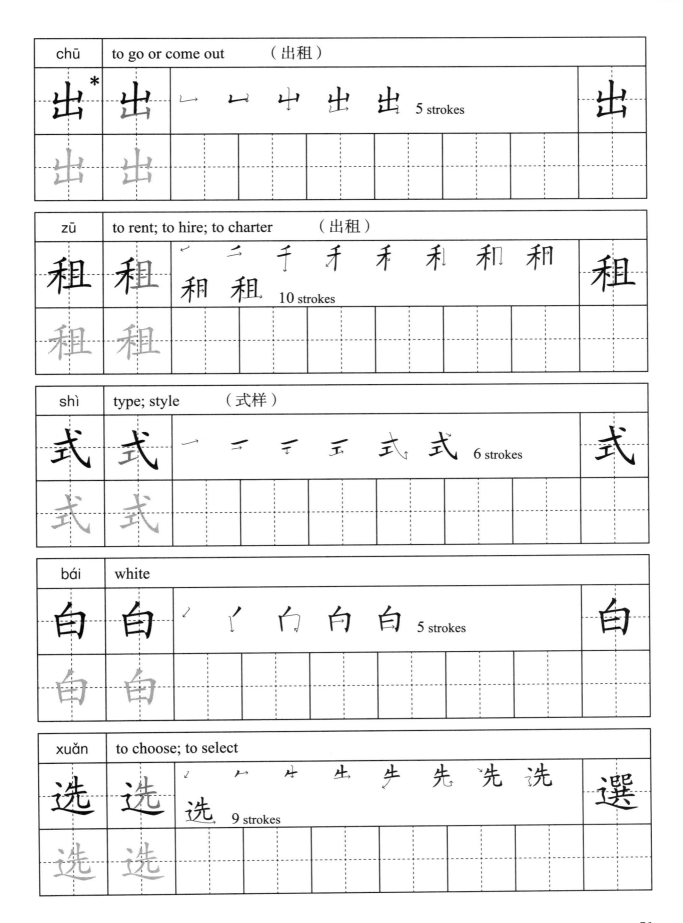

wèi	to defend; to protect	卫生 hygiene							
卫 卫	ㄱ 卫 卫 3 strokes								衛
卫 卫									

shēng	to be born; to live	卫生 hygiene							
生* 生	ノ ㇒ ⺣ 生 生 5 strokes								生
生 生									

15 Zhōngguóhuà gēn yóuhuà bù yíyàng
中国画跟油画不一样
Chinese paintings and oil paintings are different

shù	art; skill; technique （美术馆）
术	一 十 オ 木 术 5 strokes 術

kāi	to open; to start （开门）
开*	一 二 于 开 4 strokes 開

mén	door; gate; entrance （开门）
门*	丶 冂 门 3 strokes 門

hǎo	used with "好" to form "好好（儿）" (well; to one's heart's content)
好	乚 乂 女 女 奵 好 6 strokes 好

pinyin	meaning	example
zhōng	center; middle	（中国）

中* 中 丨 冂 口 中 4 strokes 中

pinyin	meaning	example
guó	country	（中国）

国* 国 丨 冂 冂 月 甲 甲 国 8 strokes 國

pinyin	meaning	example
huà	painting; to paint	（中国画）

画 画 一 厂 厅 币 禸 画 画 8 strokes 畫

pinyin	meaning	example
huā	flower	（花鸟画）

花 花 一 艹 艹 艹 艾 花 花 7 strokes 花

pinyin	meaning	example
niǎo	bird	（花鸟画）

鸟 鸟 ⺈ 勹 鸟 鸟 鸟 5 strokes 鳥

第15课　中国画跟油画不一样
Lesson 15　Chinese paintings and oil paintings are different

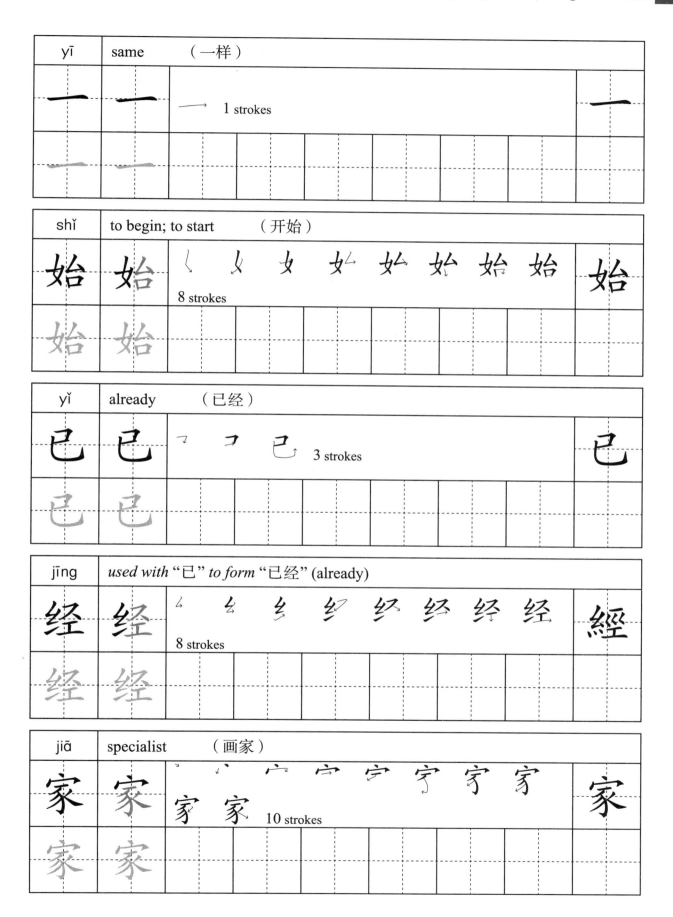

bù	not; no	（不敢）

gǎn	brave	（不敢）

dāng	to undertake	（不敢当）

yóu	oil	（油画）

duì	to	

第15课　中国画跟油画不一样
Lesson 15　Chinese paintings and oil paintings are different

gǎn	to feel; to sense　（感兴趣）

感	感	一 厂 厂 厂 后 后 咸 咸 咸 感 感 感　13 strokes	感
感	感		

xìng	interest　（兴趣）

兴*	兴	⼃ ⼀ ⺌ ⺍ 兴 兴　6 strokes	興
兴	兴		

qù	interest; delight　（兴趣）

趣	趣	一 十 土 キ キ 走 走 赶 赵 赵 趄 趄 趣 趣　15 strokes	趣
趣	趣		

jīng	capital; Beijing　（京剧）

京	京	丶 一 亠 古 亨 京 京 京　8 strokes	京
京	京		

mǎ	*used with* "虎" *to form* "马虎" (careless; casual; slipshod)

马	马	𠃍 马 马　3 strokes	馬
马	马		

qián	front
前*	9 strokes

xiē	(used to indicate an indefinite quantity) some; a few （那些）
些*	8 strokes

diàn	electricity （电梯）
电*	5 strokes 電

tī	ladder; stairs （电梯）
梯	11 strokes

xiào	to smile; to laugh （玩笑）
笑	10 strokes

第 15 课 中国画跟油画不一样
Lesson 15 Chinese paintings and oil paintings are different

mò	Chinese ink									
墨 墨		墨 墨 黑 黑 黑 墨 墨 15 strokes								墨
墨 墨										

cǎi	colour （油彩）									
彩 彩		彩 彩 彩 11 strokes								彩
彩 彩										

pǐ	a measure word for horses									
匹 匹		一 丆 兀 匹 4 strokes								匹
匹 匹										

bié	other; another （别的）									
别 别		口 口 另 另 别 7 strokes								别
别 别										

hǎo	very; quite （好像）									
好 好		乚 厶 女 好 好 好 6 strokes								好
好 好										

第 15 课　中国画跟油画不一样
Lesson 15　Chinese paintings and oil paintings are different

xiàng	to be alike; to resemble （好像）

像　像　ノ 亻 亻 伫 伫 伊 伊 伊 伊 像 像 像 像　13 strokes　像

wǎng	to; towards

往　往　ノ ノ 彳 彳 彳 行 往 往　8 strokes　往

xiā	shrimp

虾　虾　丨 口 口 中 虫 虫 虫 虾 虾　9 strokes　蝦

shū	to write （书法）

书　书　ㄋ ㄋ 书 书　4 strokes　書

dàn	but （但是）

但　但　ノ 亻 亻 但 但 但 但　7 strokes　但

jiè	to be between the two		介绍 to introduce			
介* 介	ノ 人 个 介 4 strokes						介
介 介							

shào	used with "介" to form "介绍" (to introduce)					
绍* 绍	ㄥ 幺 纟 纠 纫 绍 绍 8 strokes						绍
绍 绍							

Wǒ shì wǔ suì kāishǐ xué yóuyǒng de
我是五岁开始学游泳的
It was at age five that I first learned to swim

jiǎn	to reduce; minus （减肥）
减	11 strokes

féi	fat; greasy （减肥）
肥	8 strokes

suǒ	used with "以" to form "所以" (so)
所	8 strokes

yǐ	used with "所" to form "所以" (so)
以	4 strokes

· 67

dòng	to move; to stir	（运动）							
动*	动	一	二	云	云	云	动	6 strokes	動
动	动								

tī	to play (literally "to kick")								
踢	踢	𠃊 口 口 口 足 足 足 趵 跹 跹 跹 踢 踢 踢 15 strokes							踢
踢	踢								

zú	foot	（足球）							
足	足	丨 口 口 口 足 足 足 7 strokes							足
足	足								

qiú	ball	（足球）							
球	球	一 二 王 王 玎 玎 玎 玎 球 球 球 11 strokes							球
球	球								

bù	step; pace			跑步 to run; to jog					
步	步	丨 卜 止 止 ⺍ 步 7 strokes							步
步	步								

第16课　我是五岁开始学游泳的
Lesson 16　It was at age five that I first learned to swim

duì	team	（队员）							
队	队	乛　阝　阝　队　4 strokes							隊

yǒu	to have; there is/are								
有*	有	一　ナ　ナ　冇　有　有　6 strokes							有

yóu	to swim	（游泳）							
游*	游	丶　丶　氵　氵　氵　汸　汸　汸　浒　浒　游　游　12 strokes							游

yǒng	to swim	（游泳）							
泳*	泳	丶　丶　氵　氵　汀　汋　泳　泳　8 strokes							泳

chí	pool	（游泳池）							
池	池	丶　丶　氵　沁　池　池　6 strokes							池

| nóng | farming; agriculture | （农村） |

农 — 6 strokes — 農

| cūn | village | （农村） |

村 — 7 strokes — 村

| jiào | to teach; to instruct | （教练） |

教 — 11 strokes — 教

| liàn | to practise | （教练） |

练* — 8 strokes — 練

| hé | river | |

河 — 8 strokes — 河

第 16 课   我是五岁开始学游泳的
Lesson 16   It was at age five that I first learned to swim

bǐ	to compare; to contrast; to compete （比赛）

比　比　一　比　比　比　4 strokes　　比

sài	contest; game （比赛）

赛　赛　丶　冫　宀　宀　宀　宀　宀　寒　寒　寒　寒　赛　赛　14 strokes　　赛

shì	to look at; to view （电视）

视　视　丶　ㄋ　ネ　ネ　ネ　初　视　视　8 strokes　　视

mí	fan; enthusiast （球迷）

迷　迷　丶　丷　丷　半　米　米　迷　迷　9 strokes　　迷

zhèng	just (doing something); just now （正在）

正　正　一　丁　下　正　正　5 strokes　　正

shì	city									
市		、 亠 宀 市 市 5 strokes								市

jīng	perfect; excellent （精彩）									
精		丷 丷 半 半 米 米 米 精 精 精 精 精 精 14 strokes								精

jí	utmost; extreme									
极		一 十 才 木 札 极 极 7 strokes								極

chà	bad									
差		丷 丷 半 兰 羊 差 差 差 差 9 strokes								差

shàng	above; preceding; previous （上半场）									
上*		丨 卜 上 3 strokes								上

第 16 课　我是五岁开始学游泳的
Lesson 16　It was at age five that I first learned to swim

bàn	half	（上半场）
半* 半	丶 丶 䒑 半 半　5 strokes	半

chǎng	whole process of a game or performance	（上半场）
场 场	一 十 土 圹 场 场　6 strokes	场

fēn	point	（比分）
分 分	丿 八 分 分　4 strokes	分

xià	below; next; latter	（下半场）
下* 下	一 丅 下　3 strokes	下

shèng	leftover; remnant	
剩 剩	一 二 千 千 禾 乖 乘 乘 乘 乘 剩　12 strokes	剩

pinyin	meaning	strokes	traditional
jiē	to answer (a phone call)	接 — 11 strokes	接
dāng	to work as; to serve as; at the time or place	当 — 6 strokes	當
wài	out; outside （外援）	外 — 5 strokes	外
yuán	to help; to rescue （外援）	援 — 12 strokes	援
fǔ	to help; to assist （辅导）	辅 — 11 strokes	輔

第 16 课　我是五岁开始学游泳的
Lesson 16 It was at age five that I first learned to swim

dǎo	to instruct; to teach　　（辅导）
导 导	ㄱ ㄱ 巴 巴 导 导　6 strokes 導
导 导	

xià	to finish work or study　　（下课）
下 下	一 丅 下　3 strokes 下
下 下	

yíng	to win
赢 赢	亠 亠 亠 言 言 言 言 言 言 言 贏 贏 贏 贏 贏 赢　17 strokes 赢
赢 赢	

17

Nǐ kànguo jīngjù méiyǒu

你看过京剧没有

Have you ever seen Beijing opera

guò	*indicating a past experience*		
过	过	一 丁 寸 寸 寸 过 过　6 strokes	過
过	过		

zá	*miscellaneous; sundry; mixed* （杂技）		
杂	杂	ノ 九 九 杂 杂 杂　6 strokes	雜
杂	杂		

jì	*ability; skill* （杂技）		
技	技	一 十 扌 扩 抄 technology 技　7 strokes	技
技	技		

zǔ	*to organize; to form* （组织）		
组	组	乙 纟 纟 纠 纫 组 组　8 strokes	組
组	组		

新实用汉语课本（第3版）汉字练习册2
New Practical Chinese Reader (3rd Edition) Chinese Characters Workbook 2

zhī	to weave （组织）

织 — 8 strokes — 繊（繁体）

zhù	marked; outstanding （著名）

著 — 11 strokes

míng	famous; well-known （著名）

名 — 6 strokes

gǔ	ancient （古典）

古 — 5 strokes

diǎn	standard work of scholarship （古典）

典 — 8 strokes

第 17 课 你看过京剧没有
Lesson 17 Have you ever seen Beijing opera

bù	*a measure word for films, works of literature, etc.*

部 部 亠 亠 立 立 立 咅 咅 咅 部 部 10 strokes

ài	to love （爱情）

爱* 爱 ㇇ ⺈ ⺈ 爫 爫 爫 爫 爫 爱 爱 10 strokes

qíng	feeling; sentiment; emotion （爱情）

情 情 丨 ㇀ 忄 忄 忄 忄 忄 情 情 情 11 strokes

gǎn	to move; to touch （感人）

感 感 一 厂 厂 厂 厂 后 后 咸 咸 咸 咸 感 感 13 strokes

gū	aunt; father's sister 姑娘 (unmarried) girl

姑 姑 ㇐ ㇄ 女 女 女 妈 姑 姑 8 strokes

Pinyin	Meaning	Character	Strokes
niáng	mother; young woman （姑娘）	娘	10 strokes
jié	to associate; 结婚 to marry	结	9 strokes
hūn	to marry （结婚）	婚	11 strokes
tòng	pain; ache; hurt （痛苦）	痛	12 strokes
sǐ	to die	死	6 strokes

Lesson 17 Have you ever seen Beijing opera

第 17 课 你看过京剧没有

lí	to leave; to part from; to be away from （离开）

离 — 10 strokes — 離

jué	actor (or actress); role （主角）

角 — 7 strokes — 角

suī	used with "然" to form "虽然" (although; though)

虽 — 9 strokes — 雖

rán	used with "虽" to form "虽然" (although; though)

然 — 12 strokes — 然

hǎo	good; nice （好听）

好* — 6 strokes — 好

新实用汉语课本(第3版)汉字练习册2
New Practical Chinese Reader (3rd Edition) Chinese Characters Workbook 2

tīng	to listen	(好听)							
听*	听	丿 丨 口 口 吁 听 听 7 strokes							聽

dài	to wear								
戴	戴	一 十 土 吉 吉 吉 吉 直 直 直 直 東 東 戴 戴 戴 17 strokes							戴

miàn	face	(面具)							
面	面	一 丆 丆 丙 面 面 面 面 面 9 strokes							面

jù	utensil; tool; implement	(面具)							
具	具	丨 冂 冂 月 目 且 具 具 8 strokes							具

liǎn	face	(脸谱)							
脸	脸	丿 刀 月 月 月 阶 阶 脸 脸 脸 11 strokes							臉

第 17 课　你看过京剧没有
Lesson 17　Have you ever seen Beijing opera

pǔ	*used with "脸" to form "脸谱" (facial makeup)*

hǎi	*used with "报" to form "海报" (poster)*

bào	*used with "海" to form "海报" (poster)*

bā	*used with "蕾" to form "芭蕾" (ballet)*

lěi	*used with "芭" to form "芭蕾" (ballet)*

新实用汉语课本（第3版）汉字练习册2
New Practical Chinese Reader (3rd Edition) Chinese Characters Workbook 2

wǔ	dance
舞*	14 strokes

yuàn	hope; wish; desire （愿意）
愿	14 strokes

yì	meaning; idea; thought （愿意）
意	13 strokes

péi	to accompany
陪	10 strokes

tí	used with "琴" to form "提琴" (violin)
提	12 strokes

第 17 课　你看过京剧没有
Lesson 17　Have you ever seen Beijing opera

qín	*a general term for certain musical instruments*
琴	12 strokes

lā	to play (the violin); to pull
拉	8 strokes

hán	cold　（寒假）
寒	12 strokes

jià	vacation; holiday　（寒假）
假	11 strokes

qǔ	tune; melody　（名曲）
曲	6 strokes

18 我们爬上长城来了
Wǒmen páshang Chángchéng lái le
We have climbed up the Great Wall

yào	to want; would like （将要）
要	9 strokes

fàng	to stop (studying or working) for a certain length of time （放假）
放	8 strokes

lǚ	to travel; to journey （旅游）
旅*	10 strokes

yóu	to travel （旅游）
游	12 strokes

新实用汉语课本（第3版）汉字练习册2
New Practical Chinese Reader (3rd Edition) Chinese Characters Workbook 2

dǎ	to calculate （打算）
打	一 扌 扌 打 打 5 strokes	打

suàn	to plan （打算）
算	ノ ⺮ ⺮ ⺮ ⺮ ⺮ ⺮ ⺮ 筲 筲 筲 笪 算 算 14 strokes	算

yōu	excellent; superior （优美）
优	ノ 亻 亻 仁 优 优 6 strokes	優

sè	scene; view; scenery （景色）
色	ノ ⺈ ⺈ 夕 夕 色 6 strokes	色

ér	used with "且" to form "而且" (but also; and)
而	一 厂 厂 丙 丙 而 6 strokes	而

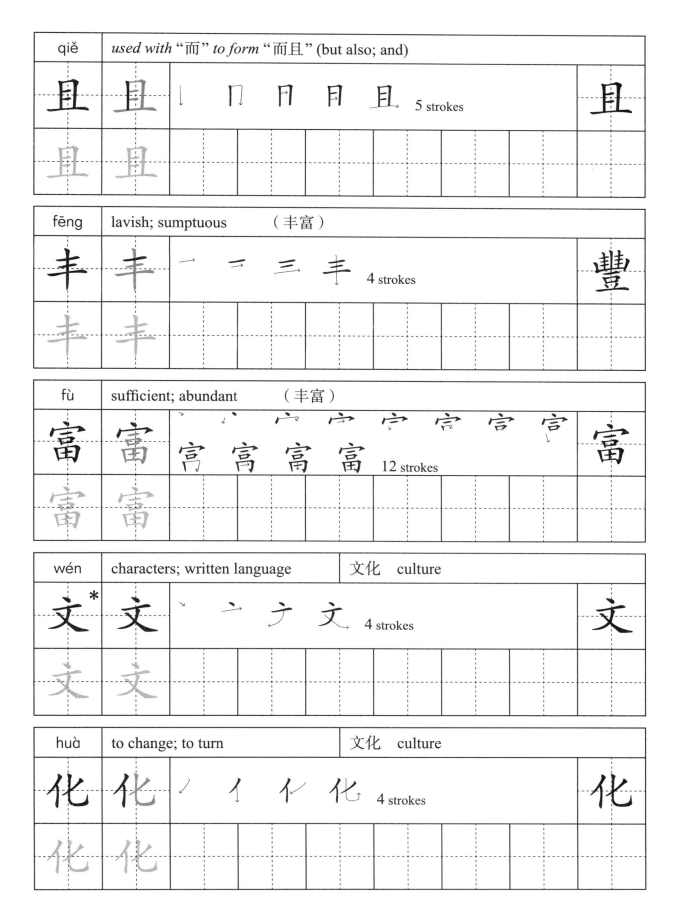

新实用汉语课本（第3版）汉字练习册2
New Practical Chinese Reader (3rd Edition) Chinese Characters Workbook 2

pá	to climb							
爬	爬	8 strokes						爬
爬	爬							

shān	hill; mountain	（山顶）						
山	山	3 strokes						山
山	山							

dǐng	peak; top	（山顶）						
顶	顶	8 strokes						顶
顶	顶							

jī	chicken	（鸡蛋）						
鸡	鸡	7 strokes						雞
鸡	鸡							

dàn	egg	（鸡蛋）						
蛋*	蛋	11 strokes						蛋
蛋	蛋							

第 18 课　我们爬上长城来了
Lesson 18　We have climbed up the Great Wall

niú	cattle; ox; cow （牛奶）

牛 　4 strokes

nǎi	milk （牛奶）

奶 　5 strokes

cài	vegetable; dish

菜 　11 strokes

lái	used after a verb, indicating the motion towards the speaker

来 　7 strokes

dòng	hole; cave （山洞）

洞 　9 strokes

新实用汉语课本(第3版)汉字练习册2
New Practical Chinese Reader (3rd Edition) Chinese Characters Workbook 2

pāi	to take (a photo) （拍照）

拍 拍 ノ 扌 扌 扩 扩 拍 拍 拍 — 8 strokes — 拍

zhào	to take (a photo) （拍照）

照 照 丨 冂 日 日 日 日 昭 昭 昭 昭 照 照 照 — 13 strokes — 照

fā	to deliver; to dispatch; to send out

发* 发 ㄥ 步 发 发 — 5 strokes — 發

yīn	overcast （阴天）

阴 阴 阝 阝 阴 阴 阴 — 6 strokes — 陰

qì	air; gas （气温）

气* 气 丿 一 气 气 — 4 strokes — 氣

96

第18课 我们爬上长城来了
Lesson 18 We have climbed up the Great Wall

wēn	temperature	（气温）								
温*	温	丶 氵 氵 氵 沪 沪 沪 沪 渭 渭 温 温 12 strokes								温
温	温									

běi	north	（北方）								
北*	北	丨 丨 十 才 北 北 5 strokes								北
北	北									

bāng	to help	（帮忙）								
帮*	帮	一 二 三 丰 丰了 邦 邦 帮 帮 9 strokes								幫
帮	帮									

máng	busy	（帮忙）								
忙*	忙	丶 丶 忄 忄 忙 忙 6 strokes								忙
忙	忙									

zhàn	to stand									
站	站	丶 亠 亠 立 立 站 站 站 站 10 strokes								站
站	站									

| qǐ | to rise; to stand up （起来） |

起 — 10 strokes

| jì | to continue; to follow （继续） |

继 — 10 strokes （繼）

| xù | to continue; to go on （继续） |

续 — 11 strokes （續）

| zhōng | to end; to finish （终于） |

终 — 8 strokes

| yú | used with "终" to form "终于" (finally) |

于 — 3 strokes

19 汽车被我撞了
Qìchē bèi wǒ zhuàng le
I crashed into a car

gē	used with "膊" to form "胳膊" (arm)

胳 — 10 strokes

bó	used with "胳" to form "胳膊" (arm)

膊 — 14 strokes

bèi	a structural particle

被 — 10 strokes

zhuàng	to hit

撞 — 15 strokes

| méi | bad luck （倒霉） |

15 strokes

| zhàn | station; stop |

10 strokes

| qí | to ride; to sit on the back of （骑车） |

11 strokes

| sī | to take charge of; to manage; to operate （司机） |

5 strokes

| jī | machine （司机） |

6 strokes

第 19 课　汽车被我撞了
Lesson 19　I crashed into a car

guǎi	to turn								
拐	拐	一 十 扌 扩 扩 护 拐 拐　8 strokes							拐
拐	拐								

zhù	to concentrate on; to fix on			注意	to pay attention to				
注	注	丶 丶 氵 氵 汁 汁 注 注　8 strokes							注
注	注								

yuán	formerly; originally	（原来）							
原	原	一 厂 厂 厂 厉 厉 百 原 原 原　10 strokes							原
原	原								

yī	to treat; to cure	（医药）							
医	医	一 二 二 三 三 天 医　7 strokes							醫
医	医								

yào	medicine	（医药）							
药*	药	一 十 艹 苁 苭 茲 药 药　9 strokes							藥
药	药								

| gòu | enough; sufficient |

够 — 11 strokes

| rú | used with "果" to form "如果" (if) |

如 — 6 strokes

| guǒ | used with "如" to form "如果" (if) |

果 — 8 strokes

| zāo | in a wretched state; bad （糟糕） |

糟 — 17 strokes

| gāo | cake　　　　糟糕　terrible; bad |

糕* — 16 strokes

第 19 课 汽车被我撞了
Lesson 19 I crashed into a car

tǎng	to lie; to recline								
躺	躺	丿 亻 白 自 自 身 身 身 身 身 躺 躺 躺 15 strokes							躺
躺	躺								

bào	newspaper	（报纸）							
报	报	一 十 扌 扩 扩 报 报 7 strokes							報
报	报								

zhǐ	paper	（报纸）							
纸	纸	乙 幺 纟 纟 纸 纸 纸 7 strokes							紙
纸	纸								

zhuō	desk; table	（桌子）							
桌	桌	丿 卜 占 占 占 卓 卓 桌 桌 10 strokes							桌
桌	桌								

jié	to end; to finish	（结果）							
结	结	乙 幺 纟 纟 纩 纩 结 结 结 9 strokes							結
结	结								

| má | hemp; any plants resembling the hemp | 麻烦 troublesome |

麻 — 11 strokes

| fán | trouble | （麻烦） |

烦 — 10 strokes

| xiāo | to eliminate; to wipe out | 消息 information; news |

消 — 10 strokes

| xī | to cease; to stop | 消息 information; news |

息* — 10 strokes

| pài | to send; to assign; to distribute | 派出所 local police station |

派 — 9 strokes

第 19 课 汽车被我撞了
Lesson 19 I crashed into a car

suǒ	office; bureau; institute （派出所）
所	8 strokes — 所

zhuā	to capture; to catch; to arrest
抓	7 strokes — 抓

yùn	luck; fate （运气）
运	7 strokes — 運

qì	spirits; morale （运气）
气	4 strokes — 氣

xīn	heart （好心）
心*	4 strokes — 心

pinyin	meaning	example	character	strokes
yīn	because; since; as; for	（因祸得福）	因	6 strokes
huò	misfortune; disaster		祸	11 strokes
dé	to get; to obtain		得	11 strokes
fú	blessing; happiness		福	13 strokes
zǎo	early	（早日）	早*	6 strokes

第 19 课　汽车被我撞了
Lesson 19　I crashed into a car

rì	day	（早日）							
日* 日		丨 冂 日 日　4 strokes							日
日 日									

kāng	health; well-being	（康复）							
康 康		丶 亠 广 广 庐 庐 庐 庚 庚 康 康　11 strokes							康
康 康									

fù	to recover; to resume	（康复）							
复 复		丿 𠂉 𠂆 ㄎ 乍 旨 复 复 复　9 strokes							復
复 复									

新实用汉语课本（第3版）汉字练习册2
New Practical Chinese Reader (3rd Edition) Chinese Characters Workbook 2

| wèi | place; location | （座位） |

位　位　ノ　亻　亻　伫　位　位　位　7 strokes　位

| guò | to cross; to pass | （过道） |

过*　过　一　十　寸　寸　过　过　6 strokes　過

| dào | road; way; path | （过道） |

道*　道　丶　丷　丷　䒑　首　首　首　首　首　道　道　12 strokes　道

| xíng | used with "李" to form "行李" (luggage; baggage) |

行　行　ノ　ノ　亻　亻　行　行　6 strokes　行

| lǐ | used with "行" to form "行李" (luggage; baggage) |

李　李　一　十　十　木　李　李　李　7 strokes　李

114

第 20 课　请把电脑拿出来
Lesson 20　Please take out your computer

tuō	to ask; to entrust	（托运）

托 托　一 亠 扌 扌 扌 托　6 strokes　托

chāo	to exceed; to surpass	（超重）

超* 超　一 亠 丄 丰 キ 圭 走 走 起 起 超 超　12 strokes　超

jīn	*jin* (500g)	（公斤）

斤* 斤　一 厂 斤 斤　4 strokes　斤

dēng	to mount; to ascend	（登机）

登 登　フ コ ヌ ヌ ダ ヅ 癶 癶 登 登 登 登　12 strokes　登

jī	plane	（登机）

机 机　一 十 才 木 机 机　6 strokes　機

pinyin	meaning		
pái	board; sign; plate	（登机牌）	牌 — 12 strokes
nǎo	brain	（电脑）	脑 — 10 strokes
xié	shoe (s)	（鞋子）	鞋 — 15 strokes
tuō	to cast off; to take off		脱 — 11 strokes
kuāng	basket		筐 — 12 strokes

第 20 课　请把电脑拿出来
Lesson 20　Please take out your computer

píng	bottle; jar; flask （瓶子）

瓶　10 strokes

āi	used to express disapproval or to remind somebody of something	哎呀 (used to express surprise) Oops!

哎　8 strokes

yā	(used to express surprise and bewilderment) ah; oh	哎呀 (used to express surprise) Oops!

呀　7 strokes

guǎng	to spread; to expand	广播　to broadcast

广　3 strokes　廣

bō	to spread	广播　to broadcast

播　15 strokes

新实用汉语课本（第3版）汉字练习册2
New Practical Chinese Reader (3rd Edition) Chinese Characters Workbook 2

dāi	to stay

liǎo	to know clearly; to understand （了解）

jiě	to understand; to comprehend （了解）

gèng	more; even more

wù	affair; business （业务）

第 20 课　请把电脑拿出来
Lesson 20　Please take out your computer

| xí | habit | （习惯） |

习　3 strokes　習

| guàn | to be accustomed to; to be in the habit of | （习惯） |

惯　11 strokes

| huó | to live | （生活） |

活　9 strokes

| wēi | minute; tiny; little | 微信　WeChat |

微　13 strokes

· 123

© 2021 北京语言大学出版社，社图号 20179

图书在版编目（CIP）数据

新实用汉语课本：英文注释．2，汉字练习册 ／ 刘
珣主编．— 3 版．— 北京：北京语言大学出版社，
2021.1
　　ISBN 978-7-5619-5784-4

　　Ⅰ.①新… Ⅱ.①刘… Ⅲ.①汉语－对外汉语教学－
习题集　Ⅳ.① H195.4

中国版本图书馆 CIP 数据核字 (2020) 第 245385 号

新实用汉语课本（第 3 版 英文注释）汉字练习册 2
XIN SHIYONG HANYU KEBEN (DI 3 BAN YINGWEN ZHUSHI) HANZI LIANXICE 2

项目负责： 付彦白	**本书策划：** 付彦白
责任编辑： 王巧燕　王世建	**英文编辑：** 侯晓娟
封面设计： 张　静	**版式设计：** 李　佳
排版制作： 北京创艺涵文化发展有限公司	
责任印制： 周　燚	

出版发行： 北京语言大学出版社

社　　址： 北京市海淀区学院路 15 号，100083

网　　址： www.blcup.com

电子信箱： service@blcup.com

电　　话： 编辑部　　8610-82303647/3592/3395
　　　　　　国内发行　8610-82303650/3591/3648
　　　　　　海外发行　8610-82303365/3080/3668
　　　　　　北语书店　8610-82303653
　　　　　　网购咨询　8610-82303908

印　　刷： 保定市中画美凯印刷有限公司

版　　次： 2021 年 1 月第 3 版　　　　**印　　次：** 2021 年 1 月第 1 次印刷

开　　本： 889 毫米 × 1194 毫米 1/16　　**印　　张：** 8.25

字　　数： 71 千字

04900

PRINTED IN CHINA